PENGUIN ⓟ CLASSICS

TWENTY LOVE POEMS
AND A SONG OF DESPAIR

PABLO NERUDA (1904–1972) was born in Parral, Chile. He grew up in the pioneer town of Temuco where he met Gabriela Mistral. In 1920 he went to Santiago to study and began to publish his poetry. In 1924 the hugely successful *Veinte poemas de amor y una canción desesperada* appeared. From 1927 to 1943 Neruda lived abroad, serving as a diplomat in Rangoon, Colombo, Batavia, Singapore, Buenos Aires, Barcelona, Madrid, Paris, and Mexico City. He joined the Communist Party of Chile after World War II, and after being prosecuted for subversion, he began a life in exile. Already the most renowned Latin American poet of his time, he returned to Chile in 1952. In accepting the Nobel Prize in 1971, he said that the poet must achieve a balance "between solitude and solidarity, between feeling and action, between intimacy of one's self, the intimacy of mankind, and the revelation of nature."

W. S. MERWIN has recieved a number of distinguished awards for his poetry—the Pulitzer Prize, the Bollingen Award, the Fellowship of the Academy of American Poets, and the Hawaiian Governor's Award for Literature among them. He has translated widely from many languages, and his versions of classics such as *The Poem of El Cid* and *The Song of Roland* are standards.

CRISTINA GARCÍA was born in Havana and grew up in New York City. She is the author of three novels—T*he Aguero Sisters*, *Dreaming in Cuban*, which was nominated for a National Book Award, and *Monkey Hunting*—and has been a Guggenheim Fellow, a Hodder Fellow at Princeton University, and the recipient of a Whiting Writers' Award.

PABLO NERUDA

Twenty Love Poems and a Song of Despair

Translated by W. S. MERWIN

Introduction by CRISTINA GARCÍA

PENGUIN BOOKS

PENGUIN BOOKS
Published by the Penguin Group
Penguin Group (USA) Inc., 375 Hudson Street, New York, New York 10014, U.S.A.
Penguin Group (Canada), 90 Eglinton Avenue East, Suite 700, Toronto,
Ontario, Canada M4P 2Y3 (a division of Pearson Penguin Canada Inc.)
Penguin Books Ltd, 80 Strand, London WC2R 0RL, England
Penguin Ireland, 25 St Stephen's Green, Dublin 2, Ireland (a division of Penguin Books Ltd)
Penguin Group (Australia), 250 Camberwell Road, Camberwell,
Victoria 3124, Australia (a division of Pearson Australia Group Pty Ltd)
Penguin Books India Pvt Ltd, 11 Community Centre, Panchsheel Park, New Delhi – 110 017, India
Penguin Group (NZ), cnr Airborne and Rosedale Roads, Albany,
Auckland 1310, New Zealand (a division of Pearson New Zealand Ltd)
Penguin Books (South Africa) (Pty) Ltd, 24 Sturdee Avenue,
Rosebank, Johannesburg 2196, South Africa

Penguin Books Ltd, Registered Offices:
80 Strand, London WC2R 0RL, England

Veínte poemas de amor y una canción desesperada first published in Chile 1924
This translation first published in Great Britain by Jonathan Cape Ltd 1969
First published in the United States of America by Grossman Publishers 1969
Published in Penguin Books 1976
Edition with an introduction by Cristina García and artwork
by Pablo Picasso published in Penguin Books 2004
This edition published 2006

23   25   27   29   30   28   26   24

English language translation copyright © W. S. Merwin, 1969
Introduction copyright © Cristina García, 2004
All rights reserved

ISBN 978-0-14-303996-9
CIP data available

Printed in the United States of America
Set in Sabon

Contents

Introduction

Body of a woman, white hills, white thighs
You look like a world, lying in surrender.
My rough peasant's body digs in you
and makes the son leap from the depth of the earth.
(FROM "BODY OF A WOMAN")

From the opening lines of this stunning collection by the twenty-year-old Pablo Neruda, it is immediately obvious that we're in the hands of a nascent master, of someone who can lead us, confidently, lyrically, from darkness into the sweet realm of the senses. That this poem, "Body of a Woman," along with twenty others, was published in 1924—when the world was still recovering from the ravages of the first truly global war—is all the more remarkable. That this collection was instantly, rapturously received signaled that the public, after being "alone in the loneliness of this hour of the dead," was hungry for a more personal, more intimate art, that they yearned for an endorsement of the individual and his struggles, loves, and losses. In Pablo Neruda, they found their poet.

Neruda arrived at the age of sixteen to the capital city of Santiago to study French literature after a childhood spent largely in Temuco, a densely forested region in the south of Chile, with his railroad worker father and his loving stepmother (Neruda's mother died of tuberculosis when he was an infant). He'd read widely and indiscriminately as a boy: the adventurous tales of Jules Verne, the sentimental novels of Victor Hugo, the pirate stories of Emilio Salgari, the experimentations of the French symbolist poets. As a teenager, he'd tried his hand at translating Baudelaire and tackled *Don Quixote*.

Neruda's family, especially his father, was opposed to his

writing poems, preferring that he concentrate on more practi-
cal pursuits. In fact, he changed his given name, Ricardo
Eliecer Neftalí Reyes, to Pablo Neruda (after the Czech histor-
ical novelist Jan Neruda) in part to avoid his father's disap-
proval. But the young Neruda could not be dissuaded from, as
he put it, "hunting poems." In a later poem in *Isla Negra*, he
described the magical natural world of his childhood:

> Rapture of the rivers,
> banks of thicket and fragrance,
> sudden boulders, burnt-out trees,
> and land, ample and lonely . . .

What emerged in *Twenty Love Poems and a Song of Despair*,
Neruda's second collection, is the voice of a poet who trusts his
senses, his curiosity, and his direct and open experience of life.
These are not abstract poems aimed at idealizing beauty or
love, but the messy, scented perceptions of lived loves—and
lusts. Neruda needed to look no further than his own world for
inspiration. His poems are populated not by distant Greek god-
desses but by the lovely, earthy Chilean women who enrap-
tured him and the solitude that frequently engulfed him.

His work is more intuitive than intellectual and his images
are firmly rooted in the severe beauty of his native soil. He con-
nects the erotic with telluric forces and the organic cycles of na-
ture. A lover becomes an "earth-shell, in whom the earth sings."
The morning star burns, "kissing our eyes." Even loss is a pro-
tagonist, goading life to its fullest expression. For all their for-
mal beauty, there is an improvised, impulsive feel to these
poems, as if they were written in the dank aftermath of pas-
sion. Transformed by memory, regrets, and above all, by his
exquisite sensibility, Neruda writes from the nuanced points
of view of his tongue and his fingertips, his nostrils, his eyes,
his ears.

> My words rained over you, stroking you.
> A long time I have loved the sunned mother-of-pearl of
>   your body.

I go so far as to think that you own the universe.
I will bring you happy flowers from the mountains,
   bluebells,
dark hazels, and rustic baskets of kisses.
I want
to do with you what spring does with the cherry trees.
   (from "Every Day You Play")

Neruda trusts and celebrates his senses and inextricably links his experiences, quite specifically, to the natural world he loves: to the damp forests of southern Chile; to the thick, gnarled roots of the pines deeply penetrating the earth; to the lonely rains that occluded the sun and cast the world through its fine veils; to the roiling rivers and seas that brought renewal and hope and, sometimes, destruction. For Neruda, this tightly woven web of nature symbolism became a grid through which he could begin to make sense of his life, to explore both the spiritual and physical worlds. For him, it was all one continuous geography.

But you, cloudless girl, question of smoke, corn tassel.
You were what the wind was making with illuminated
   leaves.
Behind the nocturnal mountains, white lily of
   conflagration,
ah, I can say nothing! You were made of everything.
   (from "Almost out of the Sky")

It is this combination of the sensory and the natural, the subjective and the eternal, the instinctual and the commonly transcendent (coupled with a fierce anti-intellectualism) that distinguishes Neruda's poetry from that of his contemporaries. He finds the glorious in the ordinary, transforming it, simply and forcefully, with his lyric genius. His preoccupation with recurring personal symbols is already in evidence in *Twenty Love Songs and a Song of Despair*: cherries and stars, rivers and roots and trains. They will forever suffuse his poetic landscape. "In the house of poetry," Neruda once declared, "nothing remains except that which was written with blood to be listened to by blood."

In Neruda's native Chile, the post-war period was marked by growing political ferment as the old, laissez-faire policy of the Parliamentary Republic (1891–1925) slowly gave way to a new constitution that not only helped erode the power of the Catholic Church but also spurred a wave of social reforms that guaranteed civil rights and social justice and established democratic-like precedents. Chileans were ready for change. They wanted their voices to be heard directly, not interpreted by others distant to their experiences. Neruda's poems spoke to this public desperate for acknowledgment.

Traditionally, many Chileans of the elite and upper-middle classes viewed themselves as European in outlook and turned to Europe, particularly France, as a guide to cultural innovation. A homegrown talent such as Neruda stirred their national pride. He spoke to them of their mountains and trees, of their rivers and nocturnal flowers, of their dreams and "the hard cold hour which the night fastens to all timetables." Neruda held up a mirror in which Chileans could view themselves and be pleased. Reading Neruda, they could feel a common identity beyond their separate lives, landmarks, and scents they could call their own. After the publication of *Twenty Love Poems and a Song of Despair*, Neruda grew famous well beyond his circle of bohemian friends in Santiago and the Chilean government rewarded him with the first of his many diplomatic postings.

Two literary figures preceded Neruda in Chile: Gabriela Mistral and Vicente Huidobro. Mistral, who knew Neruda as a schoolboy, wrote her first book of love poems in 1914, a collection that apparently had its origins in a romance with a railway employee who committed suicide. Her other early collections, which emphasized the intensity of human emotion, included *Desolación* (1922) and *Ternura* (1924) and are considered to be more hermetically personal than Neruda's poetry. Huidobro, on the other hand, was much more concerned with matters of the literary avant-garde and sought to use modern French techniques in his poetry. While admired, Huidobro's work didn't inspire in Chileans the love and close identification that Neruda's poems did.

In the world beyond Chile, postwar disillusionment and cynicism colored the collective outlook of a generation of young Europeans and Americans, one in which moral expectations were dramatically changed and the allegiances to existing social structures (government, church, moral leaders) were compromised, if not discarded. This tendency toward alienation and social dislocation was amplified by artists who pronounced the death of a discredited culture and sought fresh directions in various movements and philosophies. No more the "sleek self-satisfaction: solid, comfortable, yet decked with a faintly ironic, knowing mock-tudoring," as one critic described the Edwardian architecture of the pre–World War I years.

Though Victorian England and Europe had been characterized by optimism, security, and self-assuredness, within a few years Freud (who argued for the unconscious), Einstein (who in 1904 argued for relativity), and Heisenberg (who argued for uncertainty in 1927) unseated the categorical assumptions of the nineteenth century as delivered by Darwin's theory of evolution, Pasteur's discovery of germs, the worldwide elimination of slavery, the absence of major global conflicts for several decades, and the stranglehold of religious authority. Adding further to the sense of a general breaking down of formal structures was the advent of mass culture during the 1920s through the "talkies" and the introduction of radio and records.

Several artistic and literary movements emerged that reflected the social and philosophical crises of the times: cubism, futurism, Dadaism, ultraism, creationism, modernism, and, in the same year that Neruda published *Twenty Love Poems and a Song of Despair*, the explosion of surrealism. In one way or another, these movements were all assaults on the status quo, on realism and the constructions of national literatures, on the contention that art could be ideal and universal, that it could speak to all peoples in a unified, necessarily Western, voice.

Of these various movements, the most influential and long-standing was modernism (although in the Spanish language, *modernismo* is generally acknowledged to have begun with the

publication of Rubén Darío's *Azul* in 1888 and ended with the
Nicaraguan poet's death in 1916). Modernism flourished as it
hailed the fragmentation of daily life and the emphasis on the
individual's (usually disaffected) experience. As once-coherent
social institutions crumbled into insignificance, what was left
to relay but individual experience?

Neruda aligned himself most closely with other Latin Amer-
ican writers of his time—to the Mexican poet Ramón López
Velarde (*La sangre devota*, 1916) and the Peruvian poet César
Vallejo (*Los heraldos negros*, 1918)—who were embracing a
radical departure from their literary inheritances to an as-yet
uncharted world borne distinctly in and of the Americas. Years
later, Neruda wrote of wanting to create a poetry "corroded as
if by an acid, by the toil of the hand, impregnated with sweat
and smoke, smelling of urine and lilies."

He reminded readers that even if they'd been to hell and
back, they could still fall in love, experience beauty and rap-
ture, nurse their indignities and personal tragedies, and still ap-
preciate that "the best poet is the man who delivers our daily
bread." Neruda poignantly rendered the world of the common
man and connected him, through the redolent details of his
natural world, to forces larger than himself, forces untainted
by human crassness and ambition. His poetry challenged read-
ers to less static lives, lives susceptible to transformation, like
nature itself.

> My life grows tired, hungry to no purpose.
> I love what I do not have. You are so far.
> My loathing wrestles with the slow twilights.
> But night comes and starts to sing to me.
>
> The moon turns its clockwork dream.
> The biggest stars look at me with your eyes.
> And as I love you, the pines in the wind
> want to sing your name with their leaves of wire.
> (from "Here I Love You")

Neruda's literary contemporaries in English were trying to make sense of the world in their own ways. T. S. Eliot produced *The Wasteland* in 1922, and poets such as Hart Crane, Marianne Moore, Hilda Doolittle, Ezra Pound, William Carlos Williams, and Wallace Stevens all began their artistic ascents. Writers from other cultural traditions and literary genres were exploring the notions of unstable and indefinite identities, and that of the individual's attempt to grapple with the sudden complexities of a new world order. Among them were Luigi Pirandello, James Joyce, Fernando Pessoa, Miguel de Unamuno, Franz Kafka, Marcel Proust, Virginia Woolf, and Junichiro Tanizaki.

In short, the period following the end of World War I was not just marked by the conclusion of the war to end all wars, but also by a profound shift in the logistics of the world, from the collapse of the old system of European civilization (over six hundred years of the Austro-Hungarian Empire) to the shaky alliances that emerged after the war, from a Tsarist Russia to a Bolshevik one, from an isolationist America to a relatively more internationalist one. In 1924, Gandhi fasted for independence, Stalin succeeded Lenin, and André Breton wrote the first surrealist manifesto. When the great Spanish poet Federico García Lorca introduced Neruda to his contemporaries in Madrid a few years later, he described the Chilean as "a poet closer to death than to philosophy, a poet closer to pain than to intellect, closer to blood than to ink."

It would seem incomplete and somewhat dishonest of me to discuss *Twenty Love Poems and a Song of Despair* without commenting on the very personal impact this work has had on my life and the lives of so many of my friends. This volume was one of the first to open my eyes and sensibility to the possibility of poetry. I first read it in my late twenties (alongside Federico García Lorca and Wallace Stevens) when I was still a journalist and trying to figure out the nature of my discontent. Not only did these poems deeply resonate with me, but they galvanized me, finally, into starting to write myself. They stirred me body and soul.

With their gorgeous sweep and intimacy, their sensuality and rhapsody, and their "secret revelations of nature," Neruda's poems also made me want to reclaim Spanish, the language of my childhood, after a long, sad silence. It is not an exaggeration to say that they helped me to discover who I was and what I was meant to do. How I sang these poems aloud, again and again, in Spanish and in English, for the pure joy of hearing them on my tongue, for the imagery they conjured up and the longings they roused.

> The morning is full of storm
> in the heart of summer.
>
> The clouds travel like white handkerchiefs of good-bye,
> the wind, traveling, waving them in its hands.
>
> The numberless heart of the wind
> beating above our loving silence.
>
> Orchestral and divine, resounding among the trees
> like a language full of wars and songs.
>   (from "The Morning Is Full")

These poems have been my companions when I've fallen madly, adolescently, in love—how often have I read them to lovers, who, too, fell under their spell?—and in the bittersweet throes of break-up anguish. Like so much of Neruda's other work, these poems are meant to be spoken, shared with others. Each time I return to them, they give me something new, revitalize my perspective, and refresh and restore my senses and my sometimes-weary heart.

Whether whispering or shouting them exultantly, the poems in *Twenty Love Poems and a Song of Despair* encourage me to look closely at my own world for its small miracles and the persistence of love. They speak to me from the heart, as if for the very first time. They remind me that renewal and change are possible, cycling through life like so many seasons, inevitable and surprising at once. They do something that only

great art or faith or children, if we're lucky, do with any con-
sistency: they offer hope.

> Oh to follow the road that leads away from everything,
> without anguish, death, winter waiting along it
> with their eyes open through the dew.
>   (from "Almost out of the Sky")

—CRISTINA GARCÍA

Twenty Love Poems
and a Song of Despair

CUERPO DE MUJER

Cuerpo de mujer, blancas colinas, muslos blancos,
te pareces al mundo en tu actitud de entrega.
Mi cuerpo de labriego salvaje te socava
y hace saltar el hijo del fondo de la tierra.

Fui solo como un túnel. De mí huían los pájaros,
y en mí la noche entraba su invasión poderosa.
Para sobrevivirme te forjé como un arma,
como una flecha en mi arco, como una piedra en mi honda.

Pero cae la hora de la venganza, y te amo.
Cuerpo de piel, de musgo, de leche ávida y firme.
Ah los vasos del pecho! Ah los ojos de ausencia!
Ah las rosas del pubis! Ah tu voz lenta y triste!

Cuerpo de mujer mía, persistiré en tu gracia.
Mi sed, mi ansia, sin límite, mi camino indeciso!
Oscuros cauces donde la sed eterna sigue,
y la fatiga sigue, y el dolor infinito.

I

BODY OF A WOMAN

Body of a woman, white hills, white thighs,
you look like a world, lying in surrender.
My rough peasant's body digs in you
and makes the son leap from the depth of the earth.

I was alone like a tunnel. The birds fled from me,
and night swamped me with its crushing invasion.
To survive myself I forged you like a weapon,
like an arrow in my bow, a stone in my sling.

But the hour of vengeance falls, and I love you.
Body of skin, of moss, of eager and firm milk.
Oh the goblets of the breast! Oh the eyes of absence!
Oh the roses of the pubis! Oh your voice, slow and sad!

Body of my woman, I will persist in your grace.
My thirst, my boundless desire, my shifting road!
Dark river-beds where the eternal thirst flows
and weariness follows, and the infinite ache.

II
EN SU LLAMA MORTAL

En su llama mortal la luz te envuelve.
Absorta, pálida doliente, así situada
contra las viejas hélices del crepúsculo
que en torno a ti da vueltas.

Muda, mi amiga,
sola en lo solitario de esta hora de muertes
y llena de las vidas del fuego,
pura heredera del día destruido.

Del sol cae un racimo en tu vestido oscuro.
De la noche las grandes raíces
crecen de súbito desde tu alma,
y a lo exterior regresan las cosas en ti ocultas,
de modo que un pueblo pálido y azul
de ti recién nacido se alimenta.

Oh grandiosa y fecunda y magnética esclava
del círculo que en negro y dorado sucede:
erguida, trata y logra una creación tan viva
que sucumben sus flores, y llena es de tristeza.

THE LIGHT WRAPS YOU

The light wraps you in its mortal flame.
Abstracted pale mourner, standing that way
against the old propellers of the twilight
that revolves around you.

Speechless, my friend,
alone in the loneliness of this hour of the dead
and filled with the lives of fire,
pure heir of the ruined day.

A bough of fruit falls from the sun on your dark garment.
The great roots of night
grow suddenly from your soul,
and the things that hide in you come out again
so that a blue and pallid people,
your newly born, takes nourishment.

Oh magnificent and fecund and magnetic slave
of the circle that moves in turn through black and gold:
rise, lead and possess a creation so rich in life
that its flowers perish, and it is full of sadness.

III
AH VASTEDAD DE PINOS

Ah vastedad de pinos, rumor de olas quebrándose,
lento juego de luces, campana solitaria,
crepúsculo cayendo en tus ojos, muñeca,
caracola terrestre, en ti la tierra canta!

En ti los ríos cantan y mi alma en ellos huye
como tú lo desees y hacia donde tú quieras.
Márcame mi camino en tu arco de esperanza
y soltaré en delirio mi bandada de flechas.

En torno a mí estoy viendo tu cintura de niebla
y tu silencio acosa mis horas perseguidas,
y eres tú con tus brazos de piedra transparente
donde mis besos anclan y mi húmeda ansia anida.

Ah tu voz misteriosa que el amor tiñe y dobla
en el atardecer resonante y muriendo!
Así en horas profundas sobre los campos he visto
doblarse las espigas en la boca del viento.

AH VASTNESS OF PINES

Ah vastness of pines, murmur of waves breaking,
slow play of lights, solitary bell,
twilight falling in your eyes, toy doll,
earth-shell, in whom the earth sings!

In you the rivers sing and my soul flees in them
as you desire, and you send it where you will.
Aim my road on your bow of hope
and in a frenzy I will free my flock of arrows.

On all sides I see your waist of fog,
and your silence hunts down my afflicted hours;
my kisses anchor, and my moist desire nests
in you with your arms of transparent stone.

Ah your mysterious voice that love tolls and darkens
in the resonant and dying evening!
Thus in deep hours I have seen, over the fields,
the ears of wheat tolling in the mouth of the wind.

IV
ES LA MAÑANA LLENA

Es la mañana llena de tempestad
en el corazón del verano.

Como pañuelos blancos de adiós viajan las nubes,
el viento las sacude con sus viajeras manos.

Innumerable corazón del viento
latiendo sobre nuestro silencio enamorado.

Zumbando entre los árboles, orquestal y divino,
como una lengua llena de guerras y de cantos.

Viento que lleva en rápido robo la hojarasca
y desvía las flechas latientes de los pájaros.

Viento que la derriba en ola sin espuma
y sustancia sin peso, y fuegos inclinados.

Se rompe y se sumerge su volumen de besos
combatido en la puerta del viento del verano.

THE MORNING IS FULL

The morning is full of storm
in the heart of summer.

The clouds travel like white handkerchiefs of good-bye,
the wind, traveling, waving them in its hands.

The numberless heart of the wind
beating above our loving silence.

Orchestral and divine, resounding among the trees
like a language full of wars and songs.

Wind that bears off the dead leaves with a quick raid
and deflects the pulsing arrows of the birds.

Wind that topples her in a wave without spray
and substance without weight, and leaning fires.

Her mass of kisses breaks and sinks,
assailed in the door of the summer's wind.

PARA QUE TÚ ME OIGAS

Para que tú me oigas
mis palabras
se adelgazan a veces
como las huellas de las gaviotas en las playas.

Collar, cascabel ebrio
para tus manos suaves como las uvas.

Y las miro lejanas mis palabras.
Más que mías son tuyas.
Van trepando en mi viejo dolor como las yedras.

Ellas trepan así por las paredes húmedas.
Eres tú la culpable de este juego sangriento.
Ellas están huyendo de mi guarida oscura.
Todo lo llenas tú, todo lo llenas.

Antes que tú poblaron la soledad que ocupas,
y están acostumbradas más que tú a mi tristeza.

Ahora quiero que digan lo que quiero decirte
para que tú me oigas como quiero que me oigas.

El viento de la angustia aún las suele arrastrar.
Huracanes de sueños aún a veces las tumban.
Escuchas otras voces en mi voz dolorida.

Llanto de viejas bocas, sangre de viejas súplicas.
Ámame, compañera. No me abandones. Sígueme.
Sígueme, compañera, en esa ola de angustia.

V

SO THAT YOU WILL HEAR ME

So that you will hear me
my words
sometimes grow thin
as the tracks of the gulls on the beaches.

Necklace, drunken bell
for your hands smooth as grapes.

And I watch my words from a long way off.
They are more yours than mine.
They climb on my old suffering like ivy.

It climbs the same way on damp walls.
You are to blame for this cruel sport.
They are fleeing from my dark lair.
You fill everything, you fill everything.

Before you they peopled the solitude that you occupy,
and they are more used to my sadness than you are.

Now I want them to say what I want to say to you
to make you hear as I want you to hear me.

The wind of anguish still hauls on them as usual.
Sometimes hurricanes of dreams still knock them over.
You listen to other voices in my painful voice.

Lament of old mouths, blood of old supplications.
Love me, companion. Don't forsake me. Follow me.
Follow me, companion, on this wave of anguish.

Pero se van tiñendo con tu amor mis palabras.
Todo lo ocupas tú, todo lo ocupas.

Voy haciendo de todas un collar infinito
para tus blancas manos, suaves como las uvas.

But my words become stained with your love.
You occupy everything, you occupy everything.

I am making them into an endless necklace
for your white hands, smooth as grapes.

VI
TE RECUERDO COMO ERAS

Te recuerdo como eras en el último otoño.
Eras la boina gris y el corazón en calma.
En tus ojos peleaban las llamas del crepúsculo.
Y las hojas caían en el agua de tu alma.

Apegada a mis brazos como una enredadera,
las hojas recogían tu voz lenta y en calma.
Hoguera de estupor en que mi sed ardía.
Dulce jacinto azul torcido sobre mi alma.

Siento viajar tus ojos y es distante el otoño:
boina gris, voz de pájaro y corazón de casa
hacia donde emigraban mis profundos anhelos
y caían mis besos alegres como brasas.

Cielo desde un navío. Campo desde los cerros:
Tu recuerdo es de luz, de humo, de estanque en calma!
Más allá de tus ojos ardían los crepúsculos.
Hojas secas de otoño giraban en tu alma.

I REMEMBER YOU AS YOU WERE

I remember you as you were in the last autumn.
You were the gray beret and the still heart.
In your eyes the flames of the twilight fought on.
And the leaves fell in the water of your soul.

Clasping my arms like a climbing plant
the leaves garnered your voice, that was slow and at peace.
Bonfire of awe in which my thirst was burning.
Sweet blue hyacinth twisted over my soul.

I feel your eyes traveling, and the autumn is far off:
gray beret, voice of a bird, heart like a house
towards which my deep longings migrated
and my kisses fell, happy as embers.

Sky from a ship. Field from the hills:
Your memory is made of light, of smoke, of a still pond!
Beyond your eyes, farther on, the evenings were blazing.
Dry autumn leaves revolved in your soul.

INCLINADO EN LAS TARDES

Inclinado en las tardes tiro mis tristes redes
a tus ojos oceánicos.

Allí se estira y arde en la más alta hoguera
mi soledad que da vueltas los brazos como un náufrago.

Hago rojas señales sobre tus ojos ausentes
que olean como el mar a la orilla de un faro.

Sólo guardas tinieblas, hembra distante y mía,
de tu mirada emerge a veces la costa del espanto.

Inclinado en las tardes echo mis tristes redes
a ese mar que sacude tus ojos oceánicos.

Los pájaros nocturnos picotean las primeras estrellas
que centellean como mi alma cuando te amo.

Galopa la noche en su yegua sombría
desparramando espigas azules sobre el campo.

LEANING INTO THE AFTERNOONS

Leaning into the afternoons I cast my sad nets
towards your oceanic eyes.

There in the highest blaze my solitude lengthens
    and flames,
its arms turning like a drowning man's.

I send out red signals across your absent eyes
that move like the sea near a lighthouse.

You keep only darkness, my distant female,
from your regard sometimes the coast of dread emerges.

Leaning into the afternoons I fling my sad nets
to that sea that beats on your marine eyes.

The birds of night peck at the first stars
that flash like my soul when I love you.

The night gallops on its shadowy mare
shedding blue tassels over the land.

VIII
ABEJA BLANCA

Abeja blanca zumbas, ebria de miel, en mi alma
y te tuerces en lentas espirales de humo.

Soy el desesperado, la palabra sin ecos,
el que lo perdió todo, y el que todo lo tuvo.

Última amarra, cruje en ti mi ansiedad última.
En mi tierra desierta eres la última rosa.

Ah silenciosa!

Cierra tus ojos profundos. Allí aletea la noche.
Ah desnuda tu cuerpo de estatua temerosa.

Tienes ojos profundos donde la noche alea.
Frescos brazos de flor y regazo de rosa.

Se parecen tus senos a los caracoles blancos.
Ha venido a dormirse en tu vientre una mariposa de sombra.

Ah silenciosa!

He aquí la soledad de donde estás ausente.
Llueve. El viento del mar caza errantes gaviotas.

El agua anda descalza por las calles mojadas.
De aquel árbol se quejan, como enfermos, las hojas.

Abeja blanca, ausente, aún zumbas en mi alma.
Revives en el tiempo, delgada y silenciosa.

Ah silenciosa!

VIII

WHITE BEE

White bee, you buzz in my soul, drunk with honey,
and your flight winds in slow spirals of smoke.

I am the one without hope, the word without echoes,
he who lost everything and he who had everything.

Last hawser, in you creaks my last longing.
In my barren land you are the final rose.

Ah you who are silent!

Let your deep eyes close. There the night flutters.
Ah your body, a frightened statue, naked.

You have deep eyes in which the night flails.
Cool arms of flowers and a lap of rose.

Your breasts seem like white snails.
A butterfly of shadow has come to sleep on your belly.

Ah you who are silent!

Here is the solitude from which you are absent.
It is raining. The sea wind is hunting stray gulls.

The water walks barefoot in the wet streets.
From that tree the leaves complain as though they were sick.

White bee, even when you are gone you buzz in my soul.
You live again in time, slender and silent.

Ah you who are silent!

EBRIO DE TREMENTINA

Ebrio de trementina y largos besos,
estival, el velero de las rosas dirijo,
torcido hacia la muerte del delgado día,
cimentado en el sólido frenesí marino.

Pálido y amarrado a mi agua devorante
cruzo en el agrio olor del clima descubierto,
aún vestido de gris y sonidos amargos,
y una cimera triste de abandonada espuma.

Voy, duro de pasiones, montado en mi ola única,
lunar, solar, ardiente y frío, repentino,
dormido en la garganta de las afortunadas
islas blancas y dulces como caderas frescas.

Tiembla en la noche húmeda mi vestido de besos
locamente cargado de eléctricas gestiones,
de modo heroico dividido en sueños
y embriagadoras rosas practicándose en mí.

Aguas arriba, en medio de las olas externas,
tu paralelo cuerpo se sujeta en mis brazos
como un pez infinitamente pegado a mi alma
rápido y lento en la energía subceleste.

DRUNK WITH PINES

Drunk with pines and long kisses,
like summer I steer the fast sail of the roses,
bent towards the death of the thin day,
stuck into my solid marine madness.

Pale and lashed to my ravenous water,
I cruise in the sour smell of the naked climate,
still dressed in gray and bitter sounds
and a sad crest of abandoned spray.

Hardened by passions, I go mounted on my one wave,
lunar, solar, burning and cold, all at once,
becalmed in the throat of the fortunate isles
that are white and sweet as cool hips.

In the moist night my garment of kisses trembles
charged to insanity with electric currents,
heroically divided into dreams
and intoxicating roses practicing on me.

Upstream, in the midst of the outer waves,
your parallel body yields to my arms
like a fish infinitely fastened to my soul,
quick and slow, in the energy under the sky.

X

HEMOS PERDIDO AUN

Hemos perdido aun este crepúsculo.
Nadie nos vió esta tarde con las manos unidas
mientras la noche azul caía sobre el mundo.

He visto desde mi ventana
la fiesta del poniente en los cerros lejanos.

A veces como una moneda
se encendía un pedazo de sol entre mis manos.

Yo te recordaba con el alma apretada
de esa tristeza que tú me conoces.

Entonces, dónde estabas?
Entre qué gentes?
Diciendo qué palabras?
Por qué se me vendrá todo el amor de golpe
cuando me siento triste, y te siento lejana?

Cayó el libro que siempre se toma en el crepúsculo
y como un perro herido rodó a mis pies mi capa.

Siempre, siempre te alejas en las tardes
hacia donde el crepúsculo corre borrando estatuas.

X
WE HAVE LOST EVEN

We have lost even this twilight.
No one saw us this evening hand in hand
while the blue night dropped on the world.

I have seen from my window
the fiesta of sunset in the distant mountain tops.

Sometimes a piece of sun
burned like a coin between my hands.

I remembered you with my soul clenched
in that sadness of mine that you know.

Where were you then?
Who else was there?
Saying what?
Why will the whole of love come on me suddenly
when I am sad and feel you are far away?

The book fell that is always turned to at twilight
and my cape rolled like a hurt dog at my feet.

Always, always you recede through the evenings
towards where the twilight goes erasing statues.

CASI FUERA DEL CIELO

Casi fuera del cielo ancla entre dos montañas
la mitad de la luna.
Girante, errante noche, la cavadora de ojos.
A ver cuántas estrellas trizadas en la charca.

Hace una cruz de luto entre mis cejas, huye.
Fragua de metales azules, noches de las calladas luchas,
mi corazón da vueltas como un volante loco.
Niña venida de tan lejos, traída de tan lejos,
a veces fulgurece su mirada debajo del cielo.
Quejumbre, tempestad, remolino de furia,
cruza encima de mi corazón, sin detenerte.
Viento de los sepulcros acarrea, destroza, dispersa tu raíz
    soñolienta.

Desarraiga los grandes árboles al otro lado de ella.
Pero tú, clara niña, pregunta de humo, espiga.
Era la que iba formando el viento con hojas iluminadas.
Detrás de las montañas nocturnas, blanco lirio de incendio,
ah nada puedo decir! Era hecha de todas las cosas.

Ansiedad que partiste mi pecho a cuchillazos,
es hora de seguir otro camino, donde ella no sonría.

Tempestad que enterró las campanas, turbio revuelo de
    tormentas
para qué tocarla ahora, para qué entristecerla.

Ay seguir el camino que se aleja de todo,
donde no esté atajando la angustia, la muerte, el invierno,
con sus ojos abiertos entre el rocío.

XI

ALMOST OUT OF THE SKY

Almost out of the sky, half of the moon
anchors between two mountains.
Turning, wandering night, the digger of eyes.
Let's see how many stars are smashed in the pool.

It makes a cross of mourning between my eyes,
    and runs away.
Forge of blue metals, nights of still combats,
my heart revolves like a crazy wheel.
Girl who have come from so far, been brought from so far,
sometimes your glance flashes out under the sky.
Rumbling, storm, cyclone of fury,
you cross above my heart without stopping.
Wind from the tombs carries off, wrecks, scatters your
    sleepy root.

The big trees on the other side of her, uprooted.
But you, cloudless girl, question of smoke, corn tassel.
You were what the wind was making with illuminated leaves.
Behind the nocturnal mountains, white lily of conflagration,
ah, I can say nothing! You were made of everything.

Longing that sliced my breast into pieces,
it is time to take another road, on which she does not smile.

Storm that buried the bells, muddy swirl of torments,
why touch her now, why make her sad.

Oh to follow the road that leads away from everything,
without anguish, death, winter waiting along it
with their eyes open through the dew.

XII

PARA MI CORAZÓN

Para mi corazón basta tu pecho,
para tu libertad bastan mis alas.
Desde mi boca llegará hasta el cielo
lo que estaba dormido sobre tu alma.

Es en ti la ilusión de cada día.
Llegas como el rocío a las corolas.
Socavas el horizonte con tu ausencia.
Eternamente en fuga como la ola.

He dicho que cantabas en el viento
como los pinos y como los mástiles.
Como ellos eres alta y taciturna.
Y entristeces de pronto, como un viaje.

Acogedora como un viejo camino.
Te pueblan ecos y voces nostálgicas.
Yo desperté y a veces emigran y huyen
pájaros que dormían en tu alma.

XII

YOUR BREAST IS ENOUGH

Your breast is enough for my heart,
and my wings for your freedom.
What was sleeping above your soul will rise
out of my mouth to heaven.

In you is the illusion of each day.
You arrive like the dew to the cupped flowers.
You undermine the horizon with your absence.
Eternally in flight like the wave.

I have said that you sang in the wind
like the pines and like the masts.
Like them you are tall and taciturn,
and you are sad, all at once, like a voyage.

You gather things to you like an old road.
You are peopled with echoes and nostalgic voices.
I awoke and at times birds fled and migrated
that had been sleeping in your soul.

HE IDO MARCANDO

He ido marcando con cruces de fuego
el atlas blanco de tu cuerpo.
Mi boca era una araña que cruzaba escondiéndose.
En ti, detrás de ti, temerosa, sedienta.

Historias que contarte a la orilla del crepúsculo,
muñeca triste y dulce, para que no estuvieras triste.
Un cisne, un árbol, algo lejano y alegre.
El tiempo de las uvas, el tiempo maduro y frutal.

Yo que viví en un puerto desde donde te amaba.
La soledad cruzada de sueño y de silencio.
Acorralado entre el mar y la tristeza.
Callado, delirante, entre dos gondoleros inmóviles.

Entre los labios y la voz, algo se va muriendo.
Algo con alas de pájaro, algo de angustia y de olvido.
Así como las redes no retienen el agua.
Muñeca mía, apenas quedan gotas temblando.
Sin embargo algo canta entre estas palabras fugaces.
Algo canta, algo sube hasta mi ávida boca.
Oh poder celebrarte con todas las palabras de alegría.

Cantar, arder, huir, como un campanario en las manos de
    un loco.
Triste ternura mia, qué te haces de repente?
Cuando he llegado al vértice más atrevido y frío
mi corazón se cierra como una flor nocturna.

I HAVE GONE MARKING

I have gone marking the atlas of your body
with crosses of fire.
My mouth went across: a spider, trying to hide.
In you, behind you, timid, driven by thirst.

Stories to tell you on the shore of evening,
sad and gentle doll, so that you should not be sad.
A swan, a tree, something far away and happy.
The season of grapes, the ripe and fruitful season.

I who lived in a harbor from which I loved you.
The solitude crossed with dream and with silence.
Penned up between the sea and sadness.
Soundless, delirious, between two motionless gondoliers.

Between the lips and the voice something goes dying.
Something with the wings of a bird, something of anguish
    and oblivion.
The way nets cannot hold water.
My toy doll, only a few drops are left trembling.
Even so, something sings in these fugitive words.
Something sings, something climbs to my ravenous mouth.
Oh to be able to celebrate you with all the words of joy.

Sing, burn, flee, like a belfry at the hands of a madman.
My sad tenderness, what comes over you all at once?
When I have reached the most awesome and the coldest
    summit
my heart closes like a nocturnal flower.

JUEGAS TODO LOS DÍAS

Juegas todos los días con la luz del universo.
Sutil visitadora, llegas en la flor y en el agua.
Eres más que esta blanca cabecita que aprieto
como un racimo entre mis manos cada día.

A nadie te pareces desde que yo te amo.
Déjame tenderte entre guirnaldas amarillas.
Quién escribe tu nombre con letras de humo entre las
    estrellas del sur?
Ah déjame recordarte cómo eras entonces, cuando aún no
    existías.

De pronto el viento aúlla y golpea mi ventana cerrada.
El cielo es una red cuajada de peces sombríos.
Aquí vienen a dar todos los vientos, todos.
Se desviste la lluvia.

Pasan huyendo los pájaros.
El viento. El viento.
Yo sólo puedo luchar contra la fuerza de los hombres.
El temporal arremolina hojas oscuras
y suelta toda las barcas que anoche amarraron al cielo.

Tú estás aquí. Ah tú no huyes.
Tú me responderás hasta el último grito.
Ovíllate a mi lado como si tuvieras miedo.
Sin embargo alguna vez corrió una sombra extraña por
    tus ojos.

Ahora, ahora también, pequeña, me traes madreselvas,
y tienes hasta los senos perfumados.

EVERY DAY YOU PLAY

Every day you play with the light of the universe.
Subtle visitor, you arrive in the flower and the water.
You are more than this white head that I hold tightly
as a cluster of fruit, every day, between my hands.

You are like nobody since I love you.
Let me spread you out among yellow garlands.
Who writes your name in letters of smoke among the stars of
    the south?
Oh let me remember you as you were before you existed.

Suddenly the wind howls and bangs at my shut window.
The sky is a net crammed with shadowy fish.
Here all the winds let go sooner or later, all of them.
The rain takes off her clothes.

The birds go by, fleeing.
The wind. The wind.
I can contend only against the power of men.
The storm whirls dark leaves
and turns loose all the boats that were moored last night to
    the sky.

You are here. Oh, you do not run away.
You will answer me to the last cry.
Cling to me as though you were frightened.
Even so, at one time a strange shadow ran through your
    eyes.

Now, now too, little one, you bring me honeysuckle,
and even your breasts smell of it.

Mientras el viento triste galopa matando mariposas
yo te amo, y mi alegría muerde tu boca de ciruela.

Cuánto te habrá dolido acostumbrarte a mí,
a mi alma sola y salvaje, a mi nombre que todos ahuyen-
   tan.
Hemos visto arder tantas veces el lucero besándonos los
   ojos
y sobre nuestras cabezas destorcerse los crepúsculos en
   abanicos girantes.

Mis palabras llovieron sobre ti acariciándote.
Amé desde hace tiempo tu cuerpo de nácar soleado.
Hasta te creo dueña del universo.
Te traeré de las montañas flores alegres, copihues,
avellanas oscuras, y cestas silvestres de besos.
Quiero hacer contigo
lo que la primavera hace con los cerezos.

While the sad wind goes slaughtering butterflies
I love you, and my happiness bites the plum of your mouth.

How you must have suffered getting accustomed to me,
my savage, solitary soul, my name that sends them all
    running.
So many times we have seen the morning star burn, kissing
    our eyes,
and over our heads the grey light unwind in turning fans.

My words rained over you, stroking you.
A long time I have loved the sunned mother-of-pearl of your
    body.
I go so far as to think that you own the universe.
I will bring you happy flowers from the mountains, blue-
    bells,
dark hazels, and rustic baskets of kisses.
I want to do with you
what spring does with the cherry trees.

ME GUSTAS CUANDO CALLAS

Me gustas cuando callas porque estás como ausente,
y me oyes desde lejos, y mi voz no te toca.
Parece que los ojos se te hubieran volado
y parece que un beso te cerrara la boca.

Como todas las cosas están llenas de mi alma
emerges de las cosas, llena del alma mía.
Mariposa de sueño, te pareces a mi alma,
y te pareces a la palabra melancolía.

Me gustas cuando callas y estás como distante.
Y estás como quejándote, mariposa en arrullo.
Y me oyes desde lejos, y mi voz no te alcanza:
Déjame que me calle con el silencio tuyo.

Déjame que te hable también con tu silencio
claro como una lámpara, simple como un anillo.
Eres como la noche, callada y constelada.
Tu silencio es de estrella, tan lejano y sencillo.

Me gustas cuando callas porque estás como ausente
Distante y dolorosa como si hubieras muerto.
Una palabra entonces, una sonrisa bastan.
Y estoy alegre, alegre de que no sea cierto.

I LIKE FOR YOU
TO BE STILL

I like for you to be still: it is as though you were absent,
and you hear me from far away and my voice does not
   touch you.
It seems as though your eyes had flown away
and it seems that a kiss had sealed your mouth.

As all things are filled with my soul
you emerge from the things, filled with my soul.
You are like my soul, a butterfly of dream,
and you are like the word Melancholy.

I like for you to be still, and you seem far away.
It sounds as though you were lamenting, a butterfly cooing
   like a dove.
And you hear me from far away, and my voice does not
   reach you:
Let me come to be still in your silence.

And let me talk to you with your silence
that is bright as a lamp, simple as a ring.
You are like the night, with its stillness and constellations.
Your silence is that of a star, as remote and candid.

I like for you to be still: it is as though you were absent,
distant and full of sorrow as though you had died.
One word then, one smile, is enough.
And I am happy, happy that it's not true.

XVI

EN MI CIELO AL CREPÚSCULO

Este poema es una paráfrasis del poema 30 de
El jardinero *de Rabindranath Tagore.*

En mi cielo al crepúsculo eres como una nube
y tu color y forma son como yo los quiero.
Eres mía, eres mía, mujer de labios dulces
y viven en tu vida mis infinitos sueños.

La lámpara de mí alma te sonrosa los pies,
el agrio vino mío es más dulce en tus labios,
oh segadora de mi canción de atardecer,
cómo te sienten mía mis sueños solitarios!

Eres mía, eres mía, voy gritando en la brisa
de la tarde, y el viento arrastra mi voz viuda.
Cazadora del fondo de mis ojos, tu robo
estanca como el agua tu mirada nocturna.

En la red de mi música estás presa, amor mío,
y mis redes de música son anchas como el cielo.
Mi alma nace a la orilla de tus ojos de luto.
En tus ojos de luto comienza el país del sueño.

XVI
IN MY SKY AT TWILIGHT

*This poem is a paraphrase of the 30th poem
in Rabindranath Tagore's* The Gardener.

In my sky at twilight you are like a cloud
and your form and color are the way I love them.
You are mine, mine, woman with sweet lips
and in your life my infinite dreams live.

The lamp of my soul dyes your feet,
my sour wine is sweeter on your lips,
oh reaper of my evening song,
how solitary dreams believe you to be mine!

You are mine, mine, I go shouting it to the afternoon's
wind, and the wind hauls on my widowed voice.
Huntress of the depths of my eyes, your plunder
stills your nocturnal regard as though it were water.

You are taken in the net of my music, my love,
and my nets of music are wide as the sky.
My soul is born on the shore of your eyes of mourning.
In your eyes of mourning the land of dreams begins.

XVII
PENSANDO, ENREDANDO SOMBRAS

Pensando, enredando sombras en la profunda soledad.
Tú también estás lejos, ah más lejos que nadie.
Pensando, soltando pájaros, desvaneciendo imágenes,
enterrando lámparas.

Campanario de brumas, qué lejos, allá arriba!
Ahogando lamentos, moliendo esperanzas sombrías,
molinero taciturno,
se te viene de bruces la noche, lejos de la ciudad.

Tu presencia es ajena, extraña a mí como una cosa.
Pienso, camino largamente, mi vida antes de ti.
Mi vida antes de nadie, mi áspera vida.
El grito frente al mar, entre las piedras,
corriendo libre, loco, en el vaho del mar.
La furia triste, el grito, la soledad del mar.
Desbocado, violento, estirado hacia el cielo.

Tú, mujer, qué eras allí, qué raya, qué varilla
de ese abanico inmenso? Estabas lejos como ahora.
Incendio en el bosque! Arde en cruces azules.
Arde, arde, llamea, chispea en árboles de luz.

Se derrumba, crepita. Incendio. Incendio.
Y mi alma baila herida de virutas de fuego.
Quién llama? Qué silencio poblado de ecos?

Hora de la nostalgia, hora de la alegría, hora de la soledad,
hora mía entre todas!
Bocina en que el viento pasa cantando.
Tanta pasión de llanto anudada a mi cuerpo.

THINKING, TANGLING SHADOWS

Thinking, tangling shadows in the deep solitude.
You are far away too, oh farther than anyone.
Thinking, freeing birds, dissolving images,
burying lamps.

Belfry of fogs, how far away, up there!
Stifling laments, milling shadowy hopes,
taciturn miller,
night falls on you face downward, far from the city.

Your presence is foreign, as strange to me as a thing.
I think, I explore great tracts of my life before you.
My life before anyone, my harsh life.
The shout facing the sea, among the rocks,
running free, mad, in the sea-spray.
The sad rage, the shout, the solitude of the sea.
Headlong, violent, stretched towards the sky.

You, woman, what were you there, what ray, what vane
of that immense fan? You were as far as you are now.
Fire in the forest! Burn in blue crosses.
Burn, burn, flame up, sparkle in trees of light.

It collapses, crackling. Fire. Fire.
And my soul dances, seared with curls of fire.
Who calls? What silence peopled with echoes?

Hour of nostalgia, hour of happiness, hour of solitude,
hour that is mine from among them all!
Hunting horn through which the wind passes singing.
Such a passion of weeping tied to my body.

Sacudida de todas las raíces,
asalto de todas las olas!
Rodaba, alegre, triste interminable, mi alma.

Pensando, enterrando lámparas en la profunda soledad.

Quién eres tú, quién eres?

Shaking of all the roots,
attack of all the waves!
My soul wandered, happy, sad, unending.

Thinking, burying lamps in the deep solitude.

Who are you, who are you?

XVIII
AQUÍ TE AMO

Aquí te amo.
En los oscuros pinos se desenreda el viento.
Fosforece la luna sobre las aguas errantes.
Andan días iguales persiguiéndose.

Se desciñe la niebla en danzantes figuras.
Una gaviota de plata se descuelga del ocaso.
A veces una vela. Altas, altas, estrellas.

O la cruz negra de un barco.
Solo.
A veces amanezco, y hasta mi alma está húmeda.
Suena, resuena el mar lejano.
Éste es un puerto.
Aquí te amo.

Aquí te amo y en vano te oculta el horizonte.
Te estoy amando aún entre estas frías cosas.
A veces van mis besos en esos barcos graves,
que corren por el mar hacia donde no llegan.
Ya me veo olvidado como estas viejas anclas.
Son más triste los muelles cuando atraca la tarde.
Se fatiga mi vida inútilmente hambrienta.
Amo lo que no tengo. Estás tú tan distante.
Mi hastío forcejea con los lentos crepúsculos.
Pero la noche llega y comienza a cantarme.
La luna hace girar su rodaje de sueño.
Me miran con tus ojos las estrellas más grandes.
Y como yo te amo, los pinos en el viento,
quieren cantar tu nombre con sus hojas de alambre.

HERE I LOVE YOU

Here I love you.
In the dark pines the wind disentangles itself.
The moon glows like phosphorus on the vagrant waters.
Days, all one kind, go chasing each other.

The snow unfurls in dancing figures.
A silver gull slips down from the west.
Sometimes a sail. High, high stars.

Oh the black cross of a ship.
Alone.
Sometimes I get up early and even my soul is wet.
Far away the sea sounds and resounds.
This is a port.
Here I love you.

Here I love you and the horizon hides you in vain.
I love you still among these cold things.
Sometimes my kisses go on those heavy vessels
that cross the sea towards no arrival.
I see myself forgotten like those old anchors.
The piers sadden when the afternoon moors there.
My life grows tired, hungry to no purpose.
I love what I do not have. You are so far.
My loathing wrestles with the slow twilights.
But night comes and starts to sing to me.
The moon turns its clockwork dream.
The biggest stars look at me with your eyes.
And as I love you, the pines in the wind
want to sing your name with their leaves of wire.

XIX
NIÑA MORENA Y ÁGIL

Niña morena y ágil, el sol que hace las frutas,
el que cuaja los trigos, el que tuerce las algas,
hizo tu cuerpo alegre, tus luminosos ojos
y tu boca que tiene la sonrisa del agua.

Un sol negro y ansioso se te arrolla en las hebras
de la negra melena, cuando estiras los brazos.
Tú juegas con el sol como con un estero
y él te deja en los ojos dos oscuros remansos.

Niña morena y ágil, nada hacia ti me acerca.
Todo de ti me aleja, como del mediodía.
Eres la delirante juventud de la abeja,
la embriaguez de la ola, la fuerza de la espiga.

Mi corazón sombrío te busca, sin embargo,
y amo tu cuerpo alegre, tu voz suelta y delgada.
Mariposa morena dulce y definitiva
como el trigal y el sol, la amapola y el agua.

GIRL LITHE AND TAWNY

Girl lithe and tawny, the sun that forms
the fruits, that plumps the grains, that curls seaweeds
filled your body with joy, and your luminous eyes
and your mouth that has the smile of the water.

A black yearning sun is braided into the strands
of your black mane, when you stretch your arms.
You play with the sun as with a little brook
and it leaves two dark pools in your eyes.

Girl lithe and tawny, nothing draws me towards you.
Everything bears me farther away, as though you were noon.
You are the frenzied youth of the bee,
the drunkenness of the wave, the power of the wheat-ear.

My somber heart searches for you, nevertheless,
and I love your joyful body, your slender and flowing voice.
Dark butterfly, sweet and definitive
like the wheat-field and the sun, the poppy and the water.

PUEDO ESCRIBIR

Puedo escribir los versos más tristes esta noche.

Escribir, por ejemplo: «La noche está estrellada,
y tiritan, azules, los astros, a lo lejos.»

El viento de la noche gira en el cielo y canta.

Puedo escribir los versos más tristes esta noche.
Yo la quise, y a veces ella también me quiso.

En las noches como ésta la tuve entre mis brazos.
Le besé tantas veces bajo el cielo infinito.

Ella me quiso, a veces yo también la quería.
Cómo no haber amado sus grandes ojos fijos.

Puedo escribir los versos más tristes esta noche.
Pensar que no la tengo. Sentir que la he perdido.

Oir la noche inmensa, más inmensa sin ella.
Y el verso cae al alma como al pasto el rocío.

Qué importa que mi amor no pudiera guardarla.
La noche está estrellada y ella no está conmigo.

Eso es todo. A lo lejos alguien canta. A lo lejos.
Mi alma no se contenta con haberla perdido.

Como para acercarla mi mirada la busca.
Mi corazón la busca, y ella no está conmigo.

La misma noche que hace blanquear los mismos árboles.
Nosotros, los de entonces, ya no somos los mismos.

XX

TONIGHT I CAN WRITE

Tonight I can write the saddest lines.

Write, for example, "The night is starry
and the stars are blue and shiver in the distance."

The night wind revolves in the sky and sings.

Tonight I can write the saddest lines.
I loved her, and sometimes she loved me too.

Through nights like this one I held her in my arms.
I kissed her again and again under the endless sky.

She loved me, sometimes I loved her too.
How could one not have loved her great still eyes.

Tonight I can write the saddest lines.
To think that I do not have her. To feel that I have lost her.

To hear the immense night, still more immense without her.
And the verse falls to the soul like dew to the pasture.

What does it matter that my love could not keep her.
The night is starry and she is not with me.

This is all. In the distance someone is singing. In the distance.
My soul is not satisfied that it has lost her.

My sight tries to find her as though to bring her closer.
My heart looks for her, and she is not with me.

The same night whitening the same trees.
We, of that time, are no longer the same.

Ya no la quiero, es cierto, pero cuánto la quise.
Mi voz buscaba el viento para tocar su oído.

De otro. Será de otro. Como antes de mis besos.
Su voz, su cuerpo claro. Sus ojos infinitos.

Ya no la quiero, es cierto, pero tal vez la quiero.
Es tan corto el amor, y es tan largo el olvido.

Porque en noches como ésta la tuve entre mis brazos,
mi alma no se contenta con haberla perdido.

Aunque éste sea el último dolor que ella me causa,
y éstos sean los últimos versos que yo le escribo.

I no longer love her, that's certain, but how I loved her.
My voice tried to find the wind to touch her hearing.

Another's. She will be another's. As she was before my kisses.
Her voice, her bright body. Her infinite eyes.

I no longer love her, that's certain, but maybe I love her.
Love is so short, forgetting is so long.

Because through nights like this one I held her in my arms
my soul is not satisfied that it has lost her.

Though this be the last pain that she makes me suffer
and these the last verses that I write for her.

LA CANCIÓN DESESPERADA

Emerge tu recuerdo de la noche en que estoy.
El río anuda al mar su lamento obstinado.

Abandonado como los muelles en el alba.
Es la hora de partir, oh abandonado!

Sobre mi corazón llueven frías corolas.
Oh sentina de escombros, feroz cueva de náufragos.

En ti se acumularon las guerras y los vuelos.
De ti alzaron las alas los pájaros del canto.

Todo te lo tragaste, como la lejanía.
Como el mar, como el tiempo. Todo en ti fue naufragio!

Era la alegre hora del asalto y el beso.
La hora del estupor que ardía como un faro.

Ansiedad de piloto, furia de buzo ciego,
turbia embriaguez de amor, todo en ti fue naufragio!

En la infancia de niebla mi alma alada y herida.
Descubridor perdido, todo en ti fue naufragio!

Te ceñiste al dolor, te agarraste al deseo,
te tumbó la tristeza, todo en ti fue naufragio!

Hice retroceder la muralla de sombra,
anduve más allá del deseo y del acto.

Oh carne, carne mía, mujer que amé y perdí,
a ti en esta hora húmeda, evoco y hago canto.

Como un vaso albergaste la infinita ternura,
y el infinito olvido te trizó como a un vaso.

THE SONG OF DESPAIR

The memory of you emerges from the night around me.
The river mingles its stubborn lament with the sea.

Deserted like the wharves at dawn.
It is the hour of departure, oh deserted one!

Cold flower heads are raining over my heart.
Oh pit of debris, fierce cave of the shipwrecked.

In you the wars and the flights accumulated.
From you the wings of the song birds rose.

You swallowed everything, like distance.
Like the sea, like time. In you everything sank!

It was the happy hour of the assault and the kiss.
The hour of the spell that blazed like a lighthouse.

Pilot's dread, fury of a blind diver,
turbulent drunkenness of love, in you everything sank!

In the childhood of mist my soul, winged and wounded.
Lost discoverer, in you everything sank!

You girdled sorrow, you clung to desire,
sadness stunned you, in you everything sank!

I made the wall of shadow draw back,
beyond desire and act, I walked on.

Oh flesh, my own flesh, woman whom I loved and lost,
I summon you in the moist hour, I raise my song to you.

Like a jar you housed the infinite tenderness,
and the infinite oblivion shattered you like a jar.

Era la negra, negra soledad de las islas,
y allí, mujer de amor, me acogieron tus brazos.

Era la sed y el hambre, y tú fuiste la fruta.
Era el duelo y las ruinas, y tú fuiste el milagro.

Ah mujer, no sé cómo pudiste contenerme
en la tierra de tu alma, y en la cruz de tus brazos!

Mi deseo de ti fue el más terrible y corto,
el más revuelto y ebrio, el más tirante y ávido.

Cementerio de besos, aún hay fuego en tus tumbas,
aún los racimos arden picoteados de pájaros.

Oh la boca mordida, oh los besados miembros,
oh los hambrientos, dientes, oh los cuerpos trenzados.

Oh la cópula loca de esperanza y esfuerzo
en que nos anudamos y nos desesperamos.

Y la ternura, leve como el agua y la harina.
Y la palabra apenas comenzada en los labios.

Ese fue mi destino y en él viajó mi anhelo,
y en él cayó mi anhelo, todo en ti fue naufragio!

Oh, sentina de escombros, en ti todo caía,
qué dolor no exprimiste, qué dolor no te ahoga!

De tumbo en tumbo aún llamaste y cantaste.
De pie como un marino en la proa de un barco.

Aún floreciste en cantos, aún rompiste en corrientes.
Oh sentina de escombros, pozo abierto y amargo.

There was the black solitude of the islands,
and there, woman of love, your arms took me in.

There were thirst and hunger, and you were the fruit.
There were grief and the ruins, and you were the miracle.

Ah woman, I do not know how you could contain me
in the earth of your soul, in the cross of your arms!

How terrible and brief was my desire of you!
How difficult and drunken, how tensed and avid.

Cemetery of kisses, there is still fire in your tombs,
still the fruited boughs burn, pecked at by birds.

Oh the bitten mouth, oh the kissed limbs,
oh the hungering teeth, oh the entwined bodies.

Oh the mad coupling of hope and force
in which we merged and despaired.

And the tenderness, light as water and as flour.
And the word scarcely begun on the lips.

This was my destiny and in it was the voyage of my longing,
and in it my longing fell, in you everything sank!

Oh pit of debris, everything fell into you,
what sorrow did you not express, in what sorrow are you
    not drowned!

From billow to billow you still called and sang.
Standing like a sailor in the prow of a vessel.

You still flowered in songs, you still broke in currents.
Oh pit of debris, open and bitter well.

Pálido buzo ciego, desventurado hondero,
descubridor perdido, todo en ti fue naufragio!

Es la hora de partir, la dura y fría hora
que la noche sujeta a todo horario.

El cinturón ruidoso del mar ciñe la costa.
Surgen frías estrellas, emigran negros pájaros.

Abandonado como los muelles en el alba.
Sólo la sombra trémula se retuerce en mis manos.

Ah más allá de todo. Ah más allá de todo.

Es la hora de partir. Oh abandonado!

Pale blind diver, luckless slinger,
lost discoverer, in you everything sank!

It is the hour of departure, the hard cold hour
which the night fastens to all the timetables.

The rustling belt of the sea girdles the shore.
Cold stars heave up, black birds migrate.

Deserted like the wharves at dawn.
Only the tremulous shadow twists in my hands.

Oh farther than everything. Oh farther than everything.

It is the hour of departure. Oh abandoned one!

Selected Bibliography

A list of the principal works of Pablo Neruda with the dates of their first appearance:

La canción de la fiesta (Ediciones Juventud, Santiago, 1921)
Crepusculario (Editorial Claridad, Santiago, 1923)
Veinte poemas de amor y una canción desesperada (Nascimento, Santiago, 1924)
Tentativa del hombre infinito (Nascimento, Santiago, 1925–26)
El habitante y su esperanza (Nascimento, Santiago, 1925–26)
Anillos (Nascimento, Santiago, 1926)
El hondero entusiasta (Empresa Letras, Santiago, 1933)
Residencia en la tierra 1925–1931 (Nascimento, Santiago, 1933)
Residencia en la tierra 1925–1935 (Cruz y Raya, Madrid, 1935)
Tercera residencia 1935–1945 (Losada, Buenos Aires, 1947)
Canto general (Private Edition and Editorial Océano, Mexico, 1950)
Los versos del capitán (Private Edition, Naples, 1952)
Las uvas y el viento (Nascimento, Santiago, 1954)
Odas elementales (Losada, Buenos Aires, 1954)
Nuevas odas elementales (Losada, Buenos Aires, 1956)
Tercer libro de odas (Losada, Buenos Aires, 1957)
Obras completas (Losada, Buenos Aires, 1957; rev. and augm., 1962)
Estravagario (Losada, Buenos Aires, 1958)
Navegaciones y regresos (Losada, Buenos Aires, 1959)

Cien sonetos de amor (Private Edition, Santiago and Losada, Buenos Aires, 1959)

Cantos ceremoniales (Losada, Buenos Aires, 1961)

Plenos poderes (Losada, Buenos Aires, 1962)

Memorial de Isla Negra (Losada, Buenos Aires, 1964)

EDITOR'S NOTE: There is uncertainty, even among experts, as to some details of Neruda's bibliography.

Suggestions for Further Reading

Bestiary. Trans. Elsa Neuberger. New York: Harcourt Brace & World. 1965.

The Heights of Macchu Picchu. Trans. Nathaniel Tarn. New York: Farrar, Straus and Giroux.

Twenty Poems. Trans. Robert Bly, John Knoepfle, and James Wright. Boston, Mass.: Beacon Press. 1967.

Neruda and Vallejo: Selected Poems. Trans. Robert Bly, John Knoepfle, and James Wright. Boston, Mass.: Beacon Press. 1971.

The Captain's Verses. Trans. Donald D. Walsh. New York: New Directions. 1972.

Residence on Earth. Trans. Donald D. Walsh. New York: New Directions. 1973.

Extravagaria. Trans. Alastair Reid. New York: Farrar, Straus and Giroux. 1974.

Fully Empowered. Trans. Alastair Reid. New York: Farrar, Straus, and Giroux. 1975.

Song of Protest. Trans. Miguel Algarín. New York: William Morrow. 1976.

A Call for the Destruction of Nixon and Praise for the Chilean Revolution. Trans. Teresa Anderson. Cambridge, Mass.: West End Press. 1980.

Isla Negra: A Notebook. Trans. Alastair Reid. New York: Farrar, Straus and Giroux. 1981.

Art of Birds. Trans. Jack Schmitt. Austin: University of Texas Press. 1985.

One Hundred Love Sonnets. Trans. Stephen Tapscott. Austin: University of Texas Press. 1986.

The Stones of Chile. Trans. Dennis Maloney. Fredonia, N.Y.: White Pine Press. 1986.

Winter Garden. Trans. William O'Daly. Port Townsend, Wash.: Copper Canyon Press. 1986.

Stones of the Sky. Trans. James Nolan. Port Townsend, Wash.: Copper Canyon Press. 1987.

The Sea and the Bells. Trans. William O'Daly. Port Townsend, Wash.: Copper Canyon Press. 1988.

The Yellow Heart. Trans. William O'Daly. Port Townsend, Wash.: Copper Canyon Press. 1990.

Selected Odes of Pablo Neruda. Trans. Margaret Sayers Peden. Berkeley: University of California Press. 1991.

The Book of Questions. Trans. William O'Daly. Port Townsend, Wash.: Copper Canyon Press. 1991.

Canto General. Trans. Jack Schmitt. Berkeley: University of California Press. 1991.

2000. Trans. Richard Schaaf. Falls Church, Va.: Azul Editions. 1993.

Seaquake. Trans. María Jacketti and Dennis Maloney. Fredonia, N.Y.: White Pine Press. 1993.

CLICK ON A CLASSIC
www.penguinclassics.com

The world's greatest literature at your fingertips

Constantly updated information on more than a thousand titles, from Icelandic sagas to ancient Indian epics, Russian drama to Italian romance, American greats to African masterpieces

•

The latest news on recent additions to the list, updated editions, and specially commissioned translations

•

Original essays by leading writers

•

A wealth of background material, including biographies of every classic author from Aristotle to Zamyatin, plot synopses, readers' and teachers' guides, useful web links

•

Online desk and examination copy assistance for academics

•

Trivia quizzes, competitions, giveaways, news on forthcoming screen adaptations